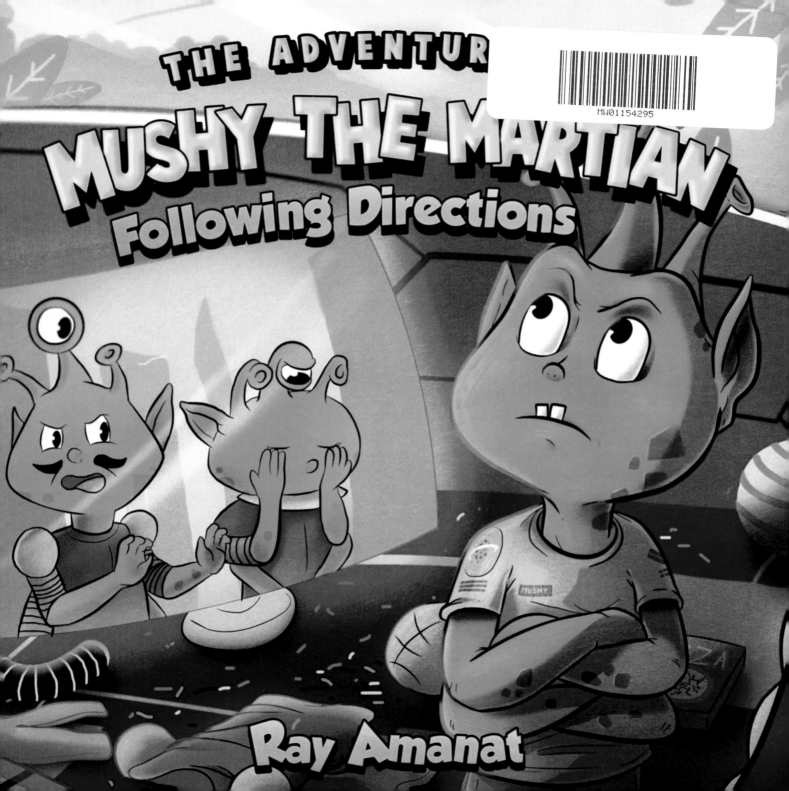

The Adventures of Mushy the Martian:Following Directions

Authored by: Ray Amanat

Copyright © 2018

Published 2018 by Paidion Publishing, Inc.

Illustrations by: Taranggana

Cover designed & layout by:Taranggana

U.S. Copyright Reg No. (Pending)

Printed in the United States of America

ISBN-13:978-1-948116-49-7

ISBN-1O:1-948116-49-9

Acknowledgement:

I'd like to thank all the teachers, counselors, social workers and parents that I have had

the privilege to work with and get insight on positive ways to help correct a child's behavior.

There are no cookie cutter strategies that work all the time as each child is unique while being

raised in different environments and coming from different cultural backgrounds.

I hope this book gives anyone that is involved in the life of a child positive solutions when

dealing with oppositional or irrational behavior.

Dedication:

I dedicate this to all the parents and teachers who have dealt with kids that have major

meltdowns or temper tantrums and are looking for a way to open a healthy discussion

to correct the child's behavior in a positive manner.

Mushy woke up from his Slumbomatic Sleep Chamber and went through his clothing closet as he threw all his other outfits on the floor until he found his favorite one.

Once he was dressed, Mushy then went to eat his favorite Martian breakfast, Klabluekey Slubergoo.
He made a mess eating and left everything there when he was done. Mushy was not used to cleaning up after himself as Mama and Papa Mush always did that for him when he lived on Mars.

Mushy got an incoming call on his video communicator from his parents. Mama Mush asked, "What's wrong with your face? You have a blimple rash and Klabluekey all over you."

Papa Mush saw all of Mushy's clothing on the floor and the mess of food on the dining table and said, "We are not on Earth to clean up after you, so you're going to have learn to do that for yourself. Here is a list of chores that we want you to learn to do so you can take better care of yourself. If you can't learn to do what's on this list, then you will have to come back to Mars."

as he stomped his feet in anger. Papa Mush wisely said, " Why don´t you ask your friends what they have to do in their homes to become healthy and strong leaders someday."

Mushy said, "My parents said that I'm too messy and gave me a list of chores to do so I can learn to be a better leader." Mushy asked his friends, "Do your parents make you do chores?"

Shasta the Shy Dog said, "My parents want me to brush my teeth, do my homework, keep my room clean, and take a bath every day. When I get older, I will have to do more chores at home. If I don't do my chores, they said that I can't hang out with my friends."

Mugsy the Mad Dog said, "My mom yells at me to do everything and I don't always listen, so I get into trouble a lot. I usually have to sit in time out until I say, 'I'm sorry' and do my chores. We never have time to do anything fun together because we're mad at each other most of the time."

Gutzy the Good Dog said, "My parents have a Star Chart with a list of chores that I'm supposed to do. For every chore that I complete without them telling me, I get a star. If I get stars on all my chores for the week, then I get to decide something fun to do with my family. If I don't get all my stars, then my parents get to decide what we do."

Mushy went back to his spaceship and told Mama and Papa Mush what he had learned from his friends. Papa Mush liked the Star Chart that Gutzy talked about and created one for Mushy.

Mama Mush said, "We want to make sure that you are ok on Earth because we love you and want the best for you. Soon you will add more chores to your Star Chart as you decide what kind of leader you want to be."

Star Chart

Responsibility / Behavior	Monday	Tuesday	Wednesday	Thursday	Friday	Saturday	Sunday	Reward
Brush Teeth								
Wash Face								
Clean Room								
Take a Bath								
Do Homework								
Read Books								

Put Dirty Laundry in Basket							
Tie your Shoes							
Use the Bathroom							
Get Dressed							

Add any other responsibility/behavior
that you would like to see an improvement in.

AUTHOR TIPS

Most elementary schools that I have presented to that have students with behavioral problems all use a point sheet or a star chart with success. The focus is more on positive reinforcement by getting the child to earn their reward rather than the negative of always threatening to take something away. The child must correct their behavior or complete their task to earn the reward agreed upon by both the parents and the child or the teacher and the child.

As adults with our careers, we get performance pay or bonuses, raises in salary, or other perks when we perform to our best abilities. Think about how those rewards make us feel when we get them and most likely celebrate those achievements.

Think about how you would celebrate your child's achievements by helping them set and accomplish realistic goals ,no matter how small or big they may be, and what it would do to build their self-esteem.

Ray Amanat Bio

Mr. Ray Amanat is the founder and curriculum coordinator for Heroes in Action®, a service based Non-profit company. His coaching focuses on character development for kids in private, public and special school districts to avoid violence and bullying in a positive, proactive way, while learning to be safe.

He is the author of, "Bully, Victim or Hero?" and a children's book series entitled, "The Adventures of Mushy the Martian". These books are teaching tools for parents and teachers to open a discussion about their child's safety. Ray wants to prevent a parent's worst nightmare, something bad happening to their child.

Mr. Amanat also speaks at corporations, colleges, and other group organizations promoting personal safety and wellness. His presentations demonstrate the benefits of simple phrases and movements that are proven to help everyone be more aware and how to escape or handle dangerous situations.

The popularity of his courses is an indication of how seriously people are taking their personal safety and the safety of their loved ones.

For more information or to get a hold of Mr. Amanat to set up
a speaking engagement or personal safety seminar, you can go to:
www.heroesinactionnow.org or call 1+ (314) 570-0243.

ISBN-13:978-1-948116-49-7
ISBN-10:1-948116-49-9

Made in the USA
Columbia, SC
08 February 2021